Wedding Guest Book

Celebrating the Marriage of

....

Wedding Date

....

Special Memories

Special Memories

Guest Name

Address and Email

....

....

....

....

Advice and Well Wishes for the Newlyweds

I hope you both..

Never forget..

Always ....

A life long marriage is built on..

My wishes for you both..

....

....

....

With love

....

Guest Name

Address and Email

....

....

....

....

Advice and Well Wishes for the Newlyweds

I hope you both ....

Never forget ....

Always ....

A life long marriage is built on ....

My wishes for you both ....

....

....

....

With love ....

Guest Name

....

Address and Email

....

....

....

Advice and Well Wishes for the Newlyweds

I hope you both..

Never forget..

Always..

A life long marriage is built on..

My wishes for you both..

....

....

....

With love

....

Guest Name

....

Address and Email

....
....
....

Advice and Well Wishes for the Newlyweds

I hope you both..

Never forget..

Always ....

A life long marriage is built on..

My wishes for you both..

....

....

....

With love ....

Special Memories

Special Memories

Guest Name

Address and Email

....

....

....

....

Advice and Well Wishes for the Newlyweds

I hope you both..

Never forget..

Always ....

A life long marriage is built on..

My wishes for you both..

....

....

....

With love

....

Guest Name

....

Address and Email

....

....

....

Advice and Well Wishes for the Newlyweds

I hope you both...

Never forget...

Always...

A life long marriage is built on...

My wishes for you both...

....

....

....

With love ....

Guest Name

....

Address and Email

....

....

....

Advice and Well Wishes for the Newlyweds

I hope you both..

Never forget..

Always ....

A life long marriage is built on.................

My wishes for you both............................

....

....

....

With love

....

Guest Name

Address and Email

....

....

....

....

Advice and Well Wishes for the Newlyweds

I hope you both ....

Never forget ....

Always ....

A life long marriage is built on ....

My wishes for you both ....

....

....

....

With love

....

Special Memories

Special Memories

Guest Name

....

Address and Email

....

....

....

Advice and Well Wishes for the Newlyweds

I hope you both..

Never forget..

Always ....

A life long marriage is built on..

My wishes for you both..

....

....

....

With love
....

Guest Name

Address and Email

....

....

....

....

Advice and Well Wishes for the Newlyweds

I hope you both..

Never forget..

Always ....

A life long marriage is built on..

My wishes for you both..

....

....

....

With love ....

Guest Name

....

Address and Email

....

....

....

Advice and Well Wishes for the Newlyweds

I hope you both..

Never forget..

Always ....

A life long marriage is built on..

My wishes for you both..

....

....

....

With love

....

Guest Name

Address and Email

....

....

....

Advice and Well Wishes for the Newlyweds

I hope you both..

Never forget...

Always ....

A life long marriage is built on...

My wishes for you both..

....

....

....

With love ....

Special Memories

Special Memories

Guest Name

Address and Email

....

....

....

....

Advice and Well Wishes for the Newlyweds

I hope you both......................................

Never forget......................................

Always ....

A life long marriage is built on......................................

My wishes for you both......................................

....

....

....

With love

....

Guest Name

....

Address and Email

....

....

....

Advice and Well Wishes for the Newlyweds

I hope you both...

Never forget...

Always ....

A life long marriage is built on...

My wishes for you both..

....

....

....

With love ....

Guest Name   Address and Email

....

                                              ....

                                              ....

Advice and Well Wishes for the Newlyweds

I hope you both...

Never forget...

Always ....

A life long marriage is built on...

My wishes for you both...

....

....

....

With love
....

Guest Name

....

Address and Email

....
....
....

Advice and Well Wishes for the Newlyweds

I hope you both................................

Never forget................................

Always ....

A life long marriage is built on................................

My wishes for you both................................

....

....

....

With love ....

Special Memories

Special Memories

Guest Name

Address and Email

....

....

....

....

Advice and Well Wishes for the Newlyweds

I hope you both...

Never forget...

Always ....

A life long marriage is built on...

My wishes for you both...

....

....

....

With love
....

Guest Name

Address and Email

....

....

....

....

Advice and Well Wishes for the Newlyweds

I hope you both..

Never forget..

Always ....

A life long marriage is built on..

My wishes for you both..

....

....

....

With love ....

Guest Name   Address and Email

....

                              ....

                              ....

Advice and Well Wishes for the Newlyweds

I hope you both..

Never forget..

Always ....

A life long marriage is built on...

My wishes for you both...

....

....

....

With love
....

Guest Name

Address and Email

....

....

....

....

Advice and Well Wishes for the Newlyweds

I hope you both...

Never forget...

Always ....

A life long marriage is built on...

My wishes for you both...

....

....

....

With love ....

Special Memories

Special Memories

Guest Name

....

Address and Email

....

....

....

Advice and Well Wishes for the Newlyweds

I hope you both...

Never forget...

Always ....

A life long marriage is built on...

My wishes for you both...

....

....

....

With love
....

Guest Name

....

Address and Email

....
....
....

Advice and Well Wishes for the Newlyweds

I hope you both...

Never forget...

Always ....

A life long marriage is built on...

My wishes for you both...

....

....

....

With love ....

Guest Name   Address and Email

....

                                              ....

                                              ....

Advice and Well Wishes for the Newlyweds

I hope you both..

Never forget...

Always ....

A life long marriage is built on...

My wishes for you both..

....

....

....

With love ....

Guest Name

....

Address and Email

....
....
....

Advice and Well Wishes for the Newlyweds

I hope you both...

Never forget...

Always ....

A life long marriage is built on..

My wishes for you both...

....

....

....

With love
....

Special Memories

Special Memories

Guest Name

Address and Email

....

....

....

....

Advice and Well Wishes for the Newlyweds

I hope you both..

Never forget..

Always ....

A life long marriage is built on..

My wishes for you both..

....

....

....

With love ....

Guest Name

....

Address and Email

....

....

....

Advice and Well Wishes for the Newlyweds

I hope you both..

Never forget..

Always ....

A life long marriage is built on..

My wishes for you both..

....

....

....

With love ....

Guest Name

Address and Email

....

....

....

....

Advice and Well Wishes for the Newlyweds

I hope you both..

Never forget..

Always ....

A life long marriage is built on..

My wishes for you both..

....

....

....

With love

....

Guest Name

Address and Email

....

....

....

....

Advice and Well Wishes for the Newlyweds

I hope you both...

Never forget...

Always ....

A life long marriage is built on...

My wishes for you both..

....

....

....

With love ....

Special Memories

Special Memories

Guest Name

....

Address and Email

....

....

....

Advice and Well Wishes for the Newlyweds

I hope you both..

Never forget..

Always ....

A life long marriage is built on......................................

My wishes for you both...

....

....

....

With love
....

Guest Name

....

Address and Email

....

....

....

Advice and Well Wishes for the Newlyweds

I hope you both...

Never forget...

Always ....

A life long marriage is built on..

My wishes for you both...

....

....

....

With love ....

Guest Name

....

Address and Email

....

....

....

Advice and Well Wishes for the Newlyweds

I hope you both..

Never forget..

Always ....

A life long marriage is built on..

My wishes for you both..

....

....

....

With love

....

Guest Name

Address and Email

....

....

....

....

Advice and Well Wishes for the Newlyweds

I hope you both..

Never forget..

Always ....

A life long marriage is built on..

My wishes for you both..

....

....

....

With love ....

Special Memories

Special Memories

Guest Name

....

Address and Email

....

....

....

Advice and Well Wishes for the Newlyweds

I hope you both..

Never forget..

Always ....

A life long marriage is built on..

My wishes for you both..

....

....

....

With love

....

Guest Name   Address and Email
....
                              ....
                              ....

Advice and Well Wishes for the Newlyweds

I hope you both..

Never forget..

Always ....

A life long marriage is built on..

My wishes for you both..

....

....

....

With love ....

Guest Name

Address and Email

....

....

....

Advice and Well Wishes for the Newlyweds

I hope you both..

Never forget..

Always ....

A life long marriage is built on..

My wishes for you both..

....

....

....

With love

....

Guest Name

....

Address and Email

....

....

....

Advice and Well Wishes for the Newlyweds

I hope you both...

Never forget...

Always ....

A life long marriage is built on...

My wishes for you both..

....

....

....

With love ....

Special Memories

Special Memories

Guest Name

....

Address and Email

....

....

....

Advice and Well Wishes for the Newlyweds

I hope you both..

Never forget..

Always ....

A life long marriage is built on..

My wishes for you both..

....

....

....

With love

....

Guest Name   Address and Email
....
                                                  ....
                                                  ....

Advice and Well Wishes for the Newlyweds

I hope you both..

Never forget..

Always ....

A life long marriage is built on..

My wishes for you both..

....

....

....

With love
....

Guest Name

....

Address and Email

....

....

....

Advice and Well Wishes for the Newlyweds

I hope you both...

Never forget...

Always ....

A life long marriage is built on............................

My wishes for you both......................................

....

....

....

With love ....

Guest Name

....

Address and Email

....

....

....

Advice and Well Wishes for the Newlyweds

I hope you both...

Never forget...

Always ....

A life long marriage is built on...

My wishes for you both...

....

....

....

With love ....

Special Memories

Special Memories

Guest Name

....

Address and Email

....
....
....

Advice and Well Wishes for the Newlyweds

I hope you both...

Never forget..

Always ....

A life long marriage is built on..

My wishes for you both...

....

....

....

With love
....

Guest Name

....

Address and Email

....
....
....

Advice and Well Wishes for the Newlyweds

I hope you both..

Never forget..

Always ....

A life long marriage is built on..

My wishes for you both..

....

....

....

With love ....

Guest Name

....

Address and Email

....

....

....

Advice and Well Wishes for the Newlyweds

I hope you both..

Never forget..

Always ....

A life long marriage is built on..

My wishes for you both..

....

....

....

With love
....

Guest Name

....

Address and Email

....

....

....

Advice and Well Wishes for the Newlyweds

I hope you both...

Never forget...

Always ....

A life long marriage is built on...

My wishes for you both..

....

....

....

With love ....

Special Memories

Special Memories

Guest Name

Address and Email

....

....

....

....

Advice and Well Wishes for the Newlyweds

I hope you both...

Never forget...

Always ....

A life long marriage is built on.................................

My wishes for you both...

....

....

....

With love

....

Guest Name

....

Address and Email

....

....

....

Advice and Well Wishes for the Newlyweds

I hope you both..

Never forget..

Always ....

A life long marriage is built on..

My wishes for you both..

....

....

....

With love ....

Guest Name

Address and Email

....

....

....

....

Advice and Well Wishes for the Newlyweds

I hope you both..

Never forget..

Always ....

A life long marriage is built on..

My wishes for you both..

....

....

....

With love

....

Guest Name

Address and Email

....

....

....

....

Advice and Well Wishes for the Newlyweds

I hope you both...

Never forget...

Always ....

A life long marriage is built on..

My wishes for you both..

....

....

....

With love ....

Guest Name

....

Address and Email

....

....

....

Advice and Well Wishes for the Newlyweds

I hope you both ....

Never forget ....

Always ....

A life long marriage is built on ....

My wishes for you both ....

....

....

....

With love ....

Guest Name

....

Address and Email

....

....

....

Advice and Well Wishes for the Newlyweds

I hope you both...

Never forget...

Always ....

A life long marriage is built on...

My wishes for you both..

....

....

....

With love ....

Gift Log

Gift	Gifted By	Thank you note sent?

Gift Log

Gift	Gifted By	Thank you note sent?
....	....	....
....	....	....
....	....	....
....	....	....
....	....	....
....	....	....
....	....	....
....	....	....
....	....	....
....	....	....
....	....	....
....	....	....
....	....	....
....	....	....
....	....	....

Gift Log

Gift	Gifted By	Thank you note sent?

Gift Log

Gift	Gifted By	Thank you note sent?

Gift Log

Gift	Gifted By	Thank you note sent?